FORTNITE BATTLE ROYALE HACKS

ADVANCED STRATEGIES FOR WINNING DUOS MATCHES

FORTNITE BATTLE ROYALE HACKS

ADVANCED STRATEGIES FOR WINNING DUOS MATCHES

AN UNOFFICIAL GUIDE TO TIPS AND TRICKS THAT OTHER GUIDES WON'T TEACH YOU

JASON R. RICH

Sky Pony Press
New York

Sky Pony Press books may be purchased in bulk at special discounts for sales promotion, corporate gifts, fund-raising, or educational purposes. Special editions can also be created to specifications. For details, contact the Special Sales Department, Sky Pony Press, 307 West 36th Street, 11th Floor, New York, NY 10018 or info@ skyhorsepublishing.com.

Sky Pony® is a registered trademark of Skyhorse Publishing, Inc.®, a Delaware corporation.

Visit our website at www.skyponypress.com.

Authors, books, and more at SkyPonyPressBlog.com.

10 9 8 7 6 5 4 3 2 1

Library of Congress Cataloging-in-Publication Data is available on file.

Series design by Brian Peterson

Print ISBN: 978-1-5107-4453-0
Ebook ISBN: 978-1-5107-4461-5

Printed in China

3930000 6272289

TABLE OF CONTENTS

FORTNITE BATTLE ROYALE HACKS

ADVANCED STRATEGIES FOR WINNING DUOS MATCHES

SECTION 1
WELCOME TO THE ISLAND

You're about to embark on an adventure like no other. You'll soon be trapped on a mysterious island and must do everything within your power to survive and ultimately achieve *#1 Victory Royale*. To accomplish this will require practice, determination, patience, and if you're playing the Duos game play mode, the ability to communicate well with your partner.

Fortnite: Battle Royale has become one of the most popular games in the world. It can be played on a PC, Mac, Xbox One, PlayStation 4, Nintendo Switch, Apple iPhone, Apple iPad, or an Android-based mobile device.

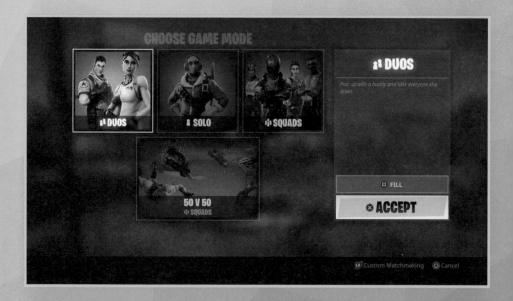

There are many reasons why *Fortnite: Battle Royale* has become so popular, with more than 125 million active players. First, it's continuously evolving. Also, each time you play *Fortnite: Battle Royale* you're able to choose between the **Solo**, **Duos**, or **Squads** game play mode. This means that every match you participate in will be different, so it never gets repetitive or boring.

The Choose Game Mode screen always offers three permanent game play modes. However, Epic Games almost always offers additional, but temporary, game play modes, such as **50 v 50 Squads** or **Playground**. Each offers a totally different experience.

Fortnite: Battle Royale Hacks—Advanced Strategies for Winning Duo Matches focuses mainly on the **Duos** game play mode, which allows you to team up with one online friend (or a random gamer), and then work together to defeat up to 98 enemy soldiers trapped with you on the mysterious island.

To make your stay on the island even more treacherous and challenging, moments after each match begins, a deadly storm (which you'll need to avoid), begins to expand across the island. The storm's impact is displayed in pink on the island map. As its intensity grows, more and more of the land becomes uninhabitable. By the end of each match, the few remaining soldiers are forced into a small area and must fight each other.

The Top 13 Tasks You'll Need to Contend with During Every Match

At the end of a match, only one soldier (or possibly two soldiers if you're playing a Duos match) will remain standing. Everyone else will perish. To survive a Duos match, you'll need to juggle a wide range of tasks throughout each exciting match, including:

1. Safely exploring the island.
2. Avoiding the deadly storm.
3. Harvesting and collecting resources (wood, stone, and metal).
4. Finding, collecting, and managing a personal arsenal of weapons.
5. Locating and collecting ammunition for the weapons.

6. Acquiring and properly using loot items that can help your soldier survive.
7. Managing the inventory within your soldier's backpack (which only has six slots capable of holding weapons and/or loot items, in addition to the pickaxe).
8. Building ramps, bridges, structures, and fortresses using collected resources in order to reach otherwise inaccessible places, or to provide defensive shielding during attacks.
9. Engaging in combat with enemy soldiers.
10. Preparing for the End Game of a match (also referred to as the *Final Circle*), when the eye of the storm is very small, and only a few of the very best soldiers remain alive.
11. Constantly communicating with your partner to plan and execute offensive and defensive strategies when it comes to fighting your enemies.
12. Exchanging and sharing weapons, ammo, loot items, and resources with your partner to ensure you enter each firefight well armed and fully prepared.
13. Reviving your partner if he or she is injured in battle, before their Health meter is fully depleted and they're eliminated from the match.

Especially during the End Game of each match, your enemies will be armed with powerful weapons and often surround you. Danger will be everywhere! You and your partner must choose the best weapons to defend yourselves, launch powerful and coordinated attacks, and ultimately defeat all who stand in your path to achieve #1 Victory Royale.

Communicating with Your Partner Is Essential!

To be successful playing *Fortnite: Battle Royale*'s Duos mode, get to know your partner's strengths and weaknesses as a gamer. Being able to effectively work together and overcome all obstacles and challenges you encounter during each match is essential. Enter into each match with the same goals and communicate throughout the match to help you efficiently achieve them.

There are several ways to communicate with your partner during a match. For example, you can use this Quick Chat menu.

If you want to share a weapon or loot item with a partner, but can't talk to them, when it's safe to do so, simply drop the weapon or item at their feet and point to it (by aiming the weapon you're holding). Your partner can then pick up what you've dropped for them.

The most effective way to communicate with your partner is for both of you to connect a gaming headset (with a built-in microphone) to your respective game systems. Doing this will allow you to talk to each other throughout the match, which makes it much easier to plan and coordinate strategies and attacks.

A Gaming Headset Is Highly Recommended!

Sound effects play an extremely important role in *Fortnite: Battle Royale*, and it's essential that you're always able to clearly hear the sound effects. For example, you can often hear the footsteps of an enemy soldier approaching, before they actually come into view.

You'll also hear the opening and closing of doors within structures, as well as the sounds of enemies using their pickaxe to smash things. As soldiers build, this too makes sound that can reveal their location. You'll also hear the unique sound chests generate. This will help you locate them if they're above or below you, or hidden behind a wall or object. Meanwhile, the sounds generated by the storm will alert you to when it's about to expand and potentially engulf you.

At the very least, play this game while wearing stereo headphones, and from the Audio Settings menu within the game, consider turning down the Music option, and turning up the Sound FX option. If you'll be playing with a partner and have a gaming headset with a built-in microphone, also turn up the Voice Chat Volume option, so you can hear everything your teammate says, even when bullets are flying and explosions are happening all around you.

Especially if you'll be playing Duos mode (or any team-oriented game play mode), using a gaming headset when experiencing a match is highly recommended. You will be able to hear the in-game sound effects the way they were meant to be heard and speak with your partner during each match. This gives you a tactical advantage, because you're able to plan strategies and coordinate detailed attacks in real-time as the action unfolds.

Turtle Beach Corp. (www.turtlebeach.com) is just one of many companies that offer high-quality gaming headsets with a built-in microphone. Plan on spending between $99.00 and $200.00 for a top-quality gaming headset, regardless of the manufacturer.

Fortnite: Battle Royale Offers Cross-Platform Compatibility

Epic Games has made *Fortnite: Battle Royale* cross-platform compatible, which means it does not matter which gaming platform you or your partner are using. You can still participate in the same matches and compete against other gamers using any compatible gaming platform. For this functionality to work, the in-game settings must be adjusted correctly.

That being said, Sony has purposely made the PS4 edition of *Fortnite: Battle Royale* incompatible with the Nintendo Switch version. As a result, if you have both of these systems, you can't use the same Epic Games account to go back and forth and play on whichever system you want. Two separate game accounts are required. You also can't play with or compete against players on a PS4 if you're using a Nintendo Switch (or vice versa).

Fortnite: Battle Royale Is Continuously Evolving

To ensure *Fortnite: Battle Royale* continues to be lit and offer ongoing challenges every time you visit the island to participate in a match, the folks at Epic Games release a game update every week or two.

A typical update includes: new weapons and/or loot items being introduced; new (unlabeled) areas being added to the island; minor alterations being made to the island's existing point of interest; and tweaks made to what existing weapons and/or loot items are capable of. Occasionally, weapons or loot items are "vaulted," meaning they're removed from the game, but could be re-introduced into the game in the future.

On a daily basis, new soldier outfits, pickaxe designs, backpack designs (called back bling), glider designs, and emotes are made available from the Item Store (shown here). These are used to customize the appearance of your soldier (but cost money). Some outfits and related items are rare or are only made available for a limited time. Anything purchased from the Item Shop is for appearances only and does not enhance the speed, strength, agility, or fighting capabilities of a soldier.

When playing a Duos game, you and your partner can have your soldiers wear the same outfit, but each of you can personalize the selected outfit with a different backpack design or pickaxe design, for example. Coordinating the appearance of your soldier needs to be done before a match.

From the Locker (shown here), choose a particularly menacing outfit that you've acquired or purchased, so you look like a well-coordinated team that will intimidate and strike fear into your rivals. While some optional outfits look comical or are theme oriented, the Flytrap and Ravel outfits are examples of "Legendary" (rare and limited-edition) outfits that will show your enemies that you mean business.

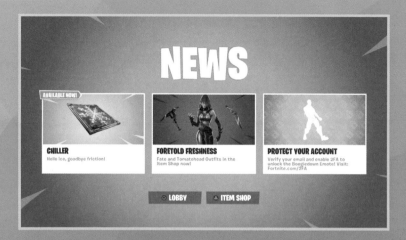

Each time something new is added to *Fortnite: Battle Royale*, a pop-up News window is displayed when you launch the game. You can also visit: www.epicgames.com/fortnite/en-US/news to discover what's new.

In addition to the weekly or biweekly updates, every three to four months, Epic Game kicks off a new game play season. In conjunction with a new season, a massive game update is released.

The start of a new season is when major new points of interest (like Paradise Palm) are added to the map, and pre-existing points of interest are dramatically altered or removed altogether. Additional changes are also made to other aspects of the game, and a new Battle Pass begins (which offers a series of daily, weekly, and tier-based challenges).

Fortnite: Battle Royale Is Free to Play

One of the things that most gamers love about *Fortnite: Battle Royale* is that it's free! Anyone, using any popular gaming platform, can download and install the game, and play on an unlimited basis for free. However, in-game purchases are required if you want to acquire items from the Item Shop, purchase a Battle Pass, or unlock Battle Pass tiers (without completing the challenges associated with each tier).

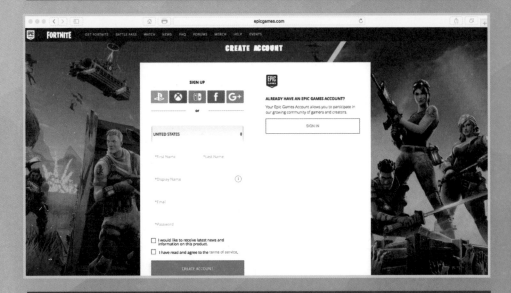

Regardless of which gaming platform you use, you'll need to set up a free Epic Games account to play *Fortnite: Battle Royale*. To create or manage your Epic Games account, visit: https://accounts.epicgames.com/register/customized. PlayStation gamers will need to link their Epic Games account to their PlayStation Network account, while Xbox One gamers will need to link their Epic Games account to their Xbox Gold Live account. Nintendo Switch gamers will need to link their Epic Games account with their My Nintendo account. Once this is done, you'll be able to find and communicate with your online friends, and partner with them to play the Duos mode of *Fortnite: Battle Royale*.

Your Adventure Is About to Begin!

Once you download and install the *Fortnite: Battle Royale* game onto your gaming system and launch the game, you'll find yourself in the Lobby. From here, select the Item Shop option to acquire new outfits and related items.

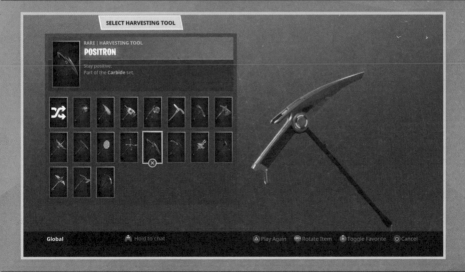

Prior to a match, access the Locker to customize your soldier using items you've purchased or have previously unlocked. One at a time, select an outfit, back bling (backpack) design, pickaxe design (shown here), glider design, contrail design, and up to six different emotes.

Access the Game Play Mode screen to choose which mode you want to experience. From this screen, after selecting a game play mode, if you've selected Duos, for example, choose between the **Fill** and **Don't Fill** option. It's found just above the Accept button. This will determine if you'll be matched up with a random gamer or be able to partner up with one of your existing online friends. From back in the Lobby, select the Play option, and the match will begin.

Your first stop is the pre-deployment area. This is where you'll meet up with your partner for the first time and wait for all the other gamers to join the match. While here, take a few moments to memorize the user-name and appearance of your partner, since you'll be working with this person throughout the match.

Depending on the skill of the gamers you're playing with and how quickly soldiers get eliminated, each match lasts approximately 15 minutes.

When playing Duos mode, your partner will always have a white arrow icon along with their username displayed above their head.

You and Your Partner Must Choose a Landing Location

While you're waiting for the Battle Bus to depart, check out the island map to see the random route the bus will be taking over the island. This is when you and your partner should choose a desired landing location. If you're both using a gaming headset, discuss where you want to land. However, if one or both of you don't have access to a headset, mark your desired landing location on the island map. The route the bus will take is displayed as a blue line (made up of arrows). This line will disappear a few moments after the Battle Bus departs.

The mysterious island you'll be landing on includes about 20 labeled areas, called points of interest. At the start of every gaming season, Epic Games adds or replaces labeled points of interest. For example, at the start of Season 5, Moisty Mire was removed, and in its place, Paradise Palms (shown here) was introduced.

Paradise Palms is a luxury area, where you're apt to discover many chests, as well as weapons, ammo, loot items, and resources lying out in the open waiting to be snatched. There are also plenty of places to explore. If the area has already been invaded by enemies, find a secure place up high (such as one of the taller buildings), and then snipe at the soldiers below.

The desert area, where Paradise Palms is located, is one of the locations on the island where you're most apt to stumble upon a Rift. Step into the Rift and you'll be catapulted into the air and be able to use your soldier's glider to navigate safely back to land. While airborne, however, you can travel a good distance quickly. In addition to Rifts, a Rift-to-Go loot item allows you to collect and use a Rift from just about anywhere on the island, when it's needed.

Anarchy Acres was replaced by Lazy Links (shown here) at the start of Season 5. This is a golf course area that offers buildings that are chock full of goodies to grab, as well as open spaces where you can drive an All Terrain Kart (ATK). Within the sand traps of the golf course, you'll often find weapons, ammo, loot items, and/or resource icons lying on the ground. Several other popular locations, like Dusty Divot, have received a makeover.

It's around Lazy Links where you'll often find All Terrain Karts (ATKs) that you can hop into and drive around. These souped-up golf carts can hold you and your partner when playing Duos mode.

The driver of an ATK can't shoot and drive at the same time, but the passenger can shoot while riding. The back of the ATK serves as a Bounce Pad, so a soldier can jump on it and fly upward to a good height and receive no injury upon landing. The driver of an ATK can honk the cart's horn. Be creative and use secret signals using the horn to communicate with your partner.

All Terrain Karts live up to their name. You can drive quickly, and go just about anywhere, including over a cliff, yet remain unharmed. Learning to perform stunts while driving an ATK takes practice. These vehicles offer the fastest way to travel around the island.

Throughout the island, in between the labeled points of interest, are many additional, albeit smaller areas to explore. If you choose to land at one of the popular points of interest, you're guaranteed to encounter enemy soldiers within seconds after landing. This will mean you need to grab a weapon and start fighting immediately, or you'll be defeated within seconds.

A smarter strategy, especially if you or your partner are not yet expert *Fortnite: Battle Royale* players, is to land in a more remote location (or just outside of a popular point of interest). Spend the first few minutes of the match avoiding enemy contact, building up your weapon arsenal, collecting ammunition, and gathering resources. This hut is located on a hill outside of Tilted Towers. You'll often discover a chest in the loft area, and/or at least one weapon or loot item on ground level.

After you've gathered some weapons and ammo, slide down the cliff and enter Tilted Towers. By waiting a few minutes after landing, many of the other soldiers who landed in the heart of this city area will have already been defeated or may have left the area, so it'll be a bit safer to explore and build up your arsenal.

Make sure your partner knows about the alternate landing spot, so he or she doesn't wind up alone in the heart of Tilted Towers, only to quickly be outnumbered, outgunned, and defeated. You can tell this happened here, because the Health meter of one soldier is at zero and there's a red marker next to their username in the top-left corner of the screen.

There are several excellent places to land on the island that are remote, and that allow you to find and gather weapons, ammo, loot items, and resources almost immediately. For example, consider landing on the roof of this tower that's been constructed on top of a house. It's located just outside of Wailing Woods (between map coordinates I2.5 and J2.5). Smash through the roof of the tower, and then explore the tower and the house to find everything there is to collect.

You'll often find up to three chests in this house/tower, along with a selection of other useful things to grab.

Smash items within the house to harvest resources, and then use your pickaxe to smash the wooden pallets outside to harvest additional wood. Smash the truck to harvest metal. Don't forget to check the house's garage—sometimes there is an ATK parked inside. Located nearby is Wailing Woods. While visiting this area, smash some of the large trees to harvest more wood and then head to the underground bunker that was introduced below Wailing Woods at the start of Season 6.

An alternate and equally remote place to land, where you're apt to quickly find many weapons, ammo, loot items, and resources to collect, is this small village located in the desert, outside of Paradise Palms (near map coordinates H9.5).

Another example of a remote place to land, where you'll find a great stash of goodies, is this large wooden tower located just outside of Lonely Lodge (between map coordinates I4.5 and J4.5). The RV park located near map coordinates I.5 and the cluster of structures at map coordinates D.8 are also potentially good landing sites if you want to initially avoid enemies and build up your arsenal.

This remote location (found near map coordinates D8) has a few structures, within which you'll find chests and plenty of other items to grab, usually without the hassle of having to fight enemies.

As soon as the Battle Bus departs, it'll transport you, your partner, and up to 98 other gamers to the island where the action will unfold. You and your partner must decide when to leap from the Battle Bus and start your freefall toward the island. If you watch and listen carefully, you'll be able to tell when your partner leaves the Battle Bus.

Upon leaping from the Battle Bus, you'll free fall toward the island. To increase your falling speed (so you can reach the island faster), use the directional controls to point your soldier downward.

You and your partner need to decide if you'll stick together throughout the entire match (unless one of you is defeated), or if you'll go your separate ways initially, and then meet up as the End Game approaches. The latter strategy makes things more challenging, because most everyone else landing on the island when playing a Duos game is paired up with someone. If you encounter enemies while you're alone, you'll probably have to contend with two enemy soldiers working together to attack you at the same time.

Anytime during the free fall, you're able to activate your soldier's glider. This is used to slow down their falling speed and give you more precise navigational control. If you don't activate the glider yourself, as your soldier gets close to land, it'll activate automatically to ensure a safe landing.

The moment you and your partner reach the island, your first two objectives should be to find and grab a weapon (and ammo), and to take cover, so you're safe from an enemy attack. Upon landing, each soldier is armed only with a pickaxe. This can be used as a close-range weapon, but it's no match for a gun or explosive. If you land in a familiar place, remember where you found chests in the past. When you return to that location in future matches, more often than not, another chest will be waiting for you.

The pickaxe is used throughout the match mainly to harvest resources (wood, stone, and metal), and to smash apart obstacles in your path. If you are forced to use it as a weapon, keep in mind it'll require several direct hits to defeat your opponent. Here, stone is being harvested by using the pickaxe to smash a rock formation.

Ideally, you want to be the first soldier to reach your desired landing location, so you can grab a weapon and defend yourself as enemies land close to you. If someone lands before you and grabs a weapon, they'll shoot and defeat you seconds after you land, while you're still basically defenseless.

Watch Out for the Storm

In addition to battling enemies, your soldier needs to stay aware of the deadly storm, which will continue to move and expand during each match.

The timer that's displayed just below the small Location Map on the main game screen tells you when the storm will be moving and expanding next. To determine which areas of the island are safe, and which have been ravaged by the storm, check the island map. These areas are displayed in pink. The outer circle on the island map shows you the eye of the storm, which is the safe area of the island that's still habitable. The inner circle (when displayed) shows you exactly where the storm will be expanding and moving to next.

Your exact position on the map is displayed as a white triangle icon. Your partner's position is displayed as a red, yellow, blue, or purple triangle. The white line shows you the quickest and safest path to follow to avoid the storm.

Set Markers as Rendezvous Points on the Island

If you and your partner get separated or can't discuss where to meet up on the island, either of you can place a marker on the island map. Here, the island map is zoomed in around Lucky Landing, and a red marker has been placed near the Asian temple located just outside of town.

When a marker is placed, a colored flare is displayed that only you and your partner can see. This marker can indicate where you both should land, or where you want to meet up during a match.

On the main game screen, if your partner is still alive, but not close to you, a directional icon along with their username is almost always displayed to help you keep tabs on their location. Throughout the match, you'll also be able to see your partner's Health and Shield meters. These are displayed in the top-left corner of the screen (when playing on most gaming systems, but the location may vary). Your soldier's Health and Shield meters are continuously displayed near the bottom-center of the screen on most gaming systems.

If you notice your partner's Health meter has turned red, this means he or she has been injured. At this point, all they can do is crawl around helplessly as their Health meter slowly depletes. They can't use a weapon or loot item. You have the ability to revive your partner and bring him or her back to health, but to do this, you must be very close to the injured soldier, and you must reach them before their Health meter is fully depleted. If you're too slow, or if an enemy reaches your partner first, your partner will be defeated and eliminated from the match. You'll then be on your own to complete the match. Here, one soldier is in the process of reviving the other. During this process, both soldiers are defenseless, since neither can use a weapon or build.

Especially for a noob, achieving #1 Victory Royale is extremely challenging without a lot of practice. As you perfect your gaming skills and get more acquainted with the game, however, you should be able to survive longer and longer during each match before getting defeated. Here, one soldier (when playing a Duos game) survived until the last few minutes of the End Game, but the team ultimately wound up in 4th place and defeated.

TEAM UP WITH A PARTNER FOR A DUOS MATCH

Participating in a Duos match requires you to team up with one other gamer, so you can face the challenges from the island and your adversaries together. Keep in mind, everyone else landing on the island is also initially paired with another gamer, so most of your firefights will be 2 vs. 2, at least until some of the soldiers on the island are defeated and teams are broken up.

One of the single most important things you can do during a Duos match is maintain communication with your partner and plan your strategies, so everything you do is well timed and perfectly coordinated. For example, when rushing an enemy target, flank your opponents from two different directions at the same time. If you don't plan to stick with your partner and work together, you might as well just play the Solo game play mode and skip the Duos mode altogether.

Ways to Choose Your Duos Partner

Once you've customized the appearance of your soldier using items unlocked or purchased and available to you from the Locker, return to the Lobby.

From the Lobby, access the Choose Game Mode screen. Select the Duos game play mode.

On the right side of the Choose Game Mode screen, just above the Accept button, select the Fill or No Fill option. If you want the game to choose a random gamer for you to partner with, select the Fill option and then hit the Accept button. However, if you want to choose whom you'll partner with for the Duos match, select the No Fill option, followed by the Accept button.

Back in the Lobby, if you selected the Fill option, press the Play button, and your match will begin. You and your partner, along with up to 98 other gamers, will soon find yourselves in the pre-deployment area waiting for the Battle Bus. After the match, you have the option to add the random player you were matched up with as an Epic Friend, so you can easily find and play with them again in the future.

There Are Two Ways to Choose an Online Friend to Partner With

There are two ways to invite others to partner with you for a Duos match. To select a friend who is part of your console-specific gaming network (such as the PlayStation Network for PS4 users or the Xbox Gold Live network or Xbox One users), if you already selected the No Fill option, from the Lobby, move the directional controls to select and highlight one of the "+" icons that are displayed to the right and left of your soldier. Since you've selected the Duos game play mode, you only need to fill one slot. Doing this allows you to access the Party Finder window.

The Party Finder (shown here for the PlayStation Network) allows you to see all of your online friends from your console-specific online network. Scroll down the list to choose whom you'd like to invite to be your Duos partner.

As each name on the Party Finder screen is highlighted, you'll see the Invite or Join option displayed to the right of their name (see the top listing). To invite another player to join you, select the Invite option. To respond to another player's invitation, select the Join option.

Once the other player has joined the party, select the Play option to begin the match.

To play with one of your Epic Friends (an online friend from the Epic Games network), from the Lobby screen, access the Game menu, and then select the Epic Friends option. (To access this menu on a PS4, for example, press the Options button on the controller. On the Nintendo Switch, press the "+" button on the controller.)

On the right side of the screen, directly below the Manage Epic Friends heading, you'll see three icons. The icon on the left is to manage your own online status. The middle icon is used to find and add new online friends, and the icon on the right allows you to adjust settings related to your friends. Scroll down your list of friends to determine who is online. A green dot will appear to the left of their username.

Highlight and then select the friend you want to invite and access the Epic Friends submenu associated with that friend.

Select the Invite to Party option for the selected friend. To respond to an invitation, select the Join Party option.

If someone else invites you to be their partner, the invitation will appear as a yellow banner that says "[Username] Invited You!" You'll see it near the center of the Lobby screen, to the right or left of your soldier. Accept the Invite and then select the Play option. You'll meet up with your partner in the pre-deployment area.

If you and/or your partner won't be using a gaming headset with a built-in microphone, use the Epic Friends Whisper option to send and receive text-based messages to communicate with your partner before a match to plan strategies.

How to Manage Your Epic Friends

To look up (find) a player who is not yet an Epic Friend, access the Game menu and select the Epic Friends option. On the right side of the screen, select the Add Friend icon. Manually enter the person's Epic Display Name or their email address to locate them on the network and then add them as a friend by selecting the Add option.

To adjust your own online status, so your Epic Friends will either see you're Online or Away, access the Epic Friends menu, and directly below the Manage Epic Friends heading, select the Online Status icon. From the Status menu (shown here), choose either Online or Away. If you choose Online, a green dot will appear next to your username, and your online friends will be able to find you and invite you to participate in *Fortnite: Battle Royale* matches. Choose Away, and your online friends will not be able to contact you while you're playing.

To determine what friend-related information you see displayed, access the Epic Friends Settings menu, and then turn on or off specific features that are listed by adding or removing a checkmark related to each option.

Once you've been paired up with a partner, select the Play option to be transported to the pre-deployment area. You'll typically have at least a minute or two to locate your partner (the soldier with a white arrow icon and username displayed above their head). Choose your landing location and chat with your partner prior to boarding the Battle Bus. The match is about to begin!

SECTION 3
DISCOVER THE ISLAND AND ITS MYSTERIES

The island where *Fortnite: Battle Royale* matches take place is always evolving.

In addition to the approximately 20 labeled points of interest on the island map, you'll discover many additional (albeit smaller) locations that are not labeled. These too are well worth visiting. Almost every week or two, when Epic Games releases a game patch, something new is added to the island map, or existing locations are altered in some minor way. This is what the island map looked like near the beginning of Season 6. Each time a new season kicks off, expect some major geographic changes to occur on the island.

You Can Learn a Lot from the Island Maps

There are several versions of the island map you need to become acquainted with.

The Location Map is continuously displayed on the screen during a match. It shows a small area of the island around your current location. Your exact location is displayed as a white triangle. If your partner is nearby, their location will be displayed as a colored triangle. Depending on which gaming platform you're using, where this map is displayed on the screen will vary. It's shown here on a PS4, in the top-right corner of the screen. You can't see the location of enemies on the map.

On the Location Map, areas in pink have already been engulfed by the storm. If you see a white line on the map, this is the path to follow to reach safety when the storm is expanding and approaching your location.

When you see a portion of the circle on the Location Map, this represents the border between what is or will soon be the unsafe storm ravaged area and the safe area of the island, based on your current location.

During the time you're in the pre-deployment area waiting to board the Battle Bus, or for the first 20 seconds or so that you're riding the bus, access the large island map to see the random route the Battle Bus will be taking over the island. Knowing this can help you and your partner choose your landing location. Use markers to display location flares for your allies. The buttons to press to set a marker are listed in the top-right corner of the screen.

Keep in mind, when the bus route cuts through the center of the island, you can reach almost any destination on the island using the navigational controls during freefall and once your soldier's glider is activated.

Checking the island map during a match reveals a lot of useful information.

Here's what you can learn from the island map during a match:

- The random route the Battle Bus will take across the island as it drops you off. This route is only displayed while you're in the pre-deployment area and for the first few seconds while aboard the Battle Bus.
- The location of each point of interest on the island.
- Your current location.
- The location of your partner if you're experiencing the Duos game play mode.
- The current location of the storm.
- Where the storm will be expanding and moving to next.
- If you or your partner have placed a marker on the map, it too will be displayed. A colored flare will also appear on the main game screen. Use the marker/flare to set a meetup location anytime during a match. Only you and your partner can see the marker/flare.

Each time the storm is about to expand and move, you'll hear a ticking sound and a warning message appears in the center of the screen (shown here). Check the timer (displayed directly below the Location Map) to determine when the storm will be expanding next.

Learn How Map Coordinates Work

When you look at the large island map, you'll discover it's divided into quadrants. Along the top of the map are the letters "A" through "J." Along the left edge of the map are the numbers "1" through "10." Each point of interest or location on the map can be found by its unique coordinates.

For example, Tilted Towers is found at map coordinates D5.5, and Snobby Shores is located at coordinates A5. At the start of Season 5, Paradise Palms replaced Moisty Mire and was centered around map coordinates I8, while Anarchy Acres was replaced by Lazy Lanes at map coordinates F2.5. The unlabeled Viking village (which contains the Viking ship) can be found on a mountaintop at map coordinates B4. This too has become a popular place to land at or visit.

Always Use the Terrain to Your Advantage

Each location on the island has its own unique terrain. There are mountains, hills, large flat areas, underground tunnels, forest areas, desert areas, city areas that contain lots of tall buildings and structures, suburban areas that contain houses and other smaller structures, factories, and junkyards, for example.

Tilted Towers is a city that contains lots of tall buildings. You'll always encounter enemies here, so be prepared for close-range firefights. If you know you'll be landing or walking into a highly congested area that's filled with enemies, go into the situation with the right collection of weapons, ammo, loot items, and resources, or know exactly where to find what you need within seconds after landing.

Once you clear a building of enemies, go to a higher level of a building, set yourself up near a window with a good view, and then snipe at enemies below using a long-range weapon. It's much safer to be higher up when in Tilted Towers, than it is to be roaming the streets at ground level.

At ground level in Tilted Towers (or anywhere else for that matter), you become a target for enemies perched above you, as well as nearby enemies also on ground level looking for a close-range firefight. They'll often hide behind large objects and then jump out to launch a surprise attack when you approach.

Anytime you go into a house or small structure, for example, if you encounter enemies inside, prepare for a close-range firefight. A pistol or shotgun should work well.

There are many locations on the island where structures are spread out over a large area. This means to travel between structures you'll need to run across open terrain. Especially if you know enemies are nearby, run (don't walk) in a random, zigzag pattern and keep jumping up and down, so you make yourself a difficult and fast-moving target to hit. In the situation shown here, the soldier wants to reach a Supply Drop that's landed out in the open. There could be enemies all around waiting to shoot at whomever approaches.

Approach the Supply Drop with extreme caution, so hopefully you don't attract anyone's attention. Quickly build walls around yourself and the Supply Drop before opening it and collecting what's inside.

This structure in Pleasant Park is located in the middle of the region. If you stand on its roof or better yet, build a fortress on top of the roof, you'll have an excellent, 360-degree view of the surrounding area. You'll be able to shoot at enemies in and around nearby buildings, as well as enemies located below you at ground level.

Within Shifty Shafts, for example, some of the main structures are above ground, but there's also a network of narrow, underground mining tunnels you'll want to explore. These tunnels have a maze-like layout, where you can't see around turns. In this situation, you'll want to tiptoe through the tunnels (to make the least amount of noise possible), and always have your weapon drawn.

Listen carefully for the sound of chests hidden behind walls within the mining tunnels of Shifty Shafts. As you explore homes or other structures elsewhere on the island (including the churches within Haunted Hills), you'll also hear the sound of chests, in many cases before the chests come into view. You may need to smash a wall, floor, or ceiling in order to reveal a hidden chest. Here, you can see the glow from the chest seeping through the wooden planks of the wall.

The junkyard areas (like Junk Junction) as well as the RV parks and cargo container storage facilities found throughout the island also create a maze-like layout when you're on ground level. You're better off getting to the top of the junk piles, cargo containers, or RVs so you have a height advantage and will be able to see and shoot at enemies from above.

Another way to take out enemies who are exploring at ground level in these maze-like areas is to plant Traps or Remote Explosives, for example, to boobytrap an area. Since your enemies won't be able to see around turns, they'll likely walk right into your Trap and go boom!

If you place a Trap out in the open, your enemies will likely be smart enough to avoid it. However, if you surround it with walls and a ceiling (so it looks like a fort), close the door and place an item that's useful by the door as bait, chances are an enemy will try to explore your fort and will get caught up by the Trap.

During any firefight, having a height advantage will always be beneficial. Thus, it may be necessary to quickly build a ramp and travel upward to gain the height advantage. When you do this, keep in mind that an enemy can shoot the bottom or mid-section of a tall ramp, and it'll collapse. If this happens, you'll go crashing to the ground. This could result in injury or defeat, depending on how far you fall.

When you're driving an All Terrain Kart (ATK), hills and cliffs make riding in one of these vehicles even more exciting. You can ride up most steep mountains and hills, drive over cliffs and go airborne, or in many cases smash through smaller obstacles in your path.

Anytime you're in an open body of water, whether it's Loot Lake, the smaller lake in Lazy Lanes, or a lake located outside of Paradise Palms, you'll discover that traveling through water is slow, and leaves you vulnerable to attack.

To speed up your travel through water, keep jumping up and down while moving forward. A better option is to build a wooden bridge over the water. Not only will you travel faster, but if someone starts shooting at you, you can quickly build walls around yourself for protection.

At the start of a match, the popular points of interest are always crowded with enemies. If you land outside of a popular area and quickly grab a long-range weapon, you can often find a hill or mountain that overlooks a point of interest, and then snipe at enemies from a distance. A sniper rifle or Rocket Launcher works best for this, but they're not always available when you need them.

When traveling in between points of interest, unless you're trying to outrun the storm, take the time to harvest resources by smashing trees (for wood), rock formations (for stone), vehicles (for metal), and other objects along your route.

To quickly cross between the rooftops of nearby buildings, for example, build a wooden bridge to avoid having to go to ground level and give up your height advantage.

Hiding Behind Some Objects Offers Protection Against Incoming Attacks

Wherever you happen to be on the island, use your natural surroundings to your advantage. For example, you can climb up onto something to gain a height advantage or hide behind something for protection. Try to discover creative ways to use your natural surroundings.

It's always safer to keep a little bit of distance between yourself and your partner. Otherwise, one explosive weapon or well-coordinated enemy attack could defeat you both at the same time. If you're a slight distance apart, there's always a chance that one soldier can revive his or her partner if someone gets injured.

When you're traveling on foot, you always have the option to use nearby objects as shielding from an incoming attack or to hide from enemies in hopes of avoiding a confrontation. Some objects, like a vehicle (car, bus, truck, or RV), are made of metal and provide excellent shielding if you crouch behind them.

Hiding behind a rock formation also provides decent shielding against an incoming attack.

Other objects, like haystacks, provide a place to hide behind, but no protection whatsoever if someone starts shooting at you. With one bullet hit, the haystack will be destroyed, and you'll be vulnerable.

Hiding within a bush can keep you from being seen. However, if an enemy figures out where you're hiding, that bush offers zero protection. Using the Bush loot item, however, allows you to surround yourself with the bush and move around. You'll truly blend in with your surroundings when you're outside and standing still. (Shown on an iPad Pro.)

Here, a soldier is completely surrounded by the bush and can't be seen. (Shown on an iPad Pro.)

If you can't find an object to hide behind, consider building a bunch of pyramid-shaped tiles above and all around you for protection. These are made of wood, but they'd offer much better protection if they were constructed from stone or metal.

Within a home or other structure, you can hide behind furniture. If you surprise an enemy and launch an attack first, the furniture will work to your advantage. However, if the enemy starts shooting, the furniture will offer little protection against bullets or explosives.

FINDING, COLLECTING, AND USING WEAPONS AND LOOT ITEMS

The Backpack Inventory screen allows you to see everything your soldier is carrying at any given time and to learn more about a particular weapon or ammo type. From this screen, you're also able to re-organize which backpack slot a particular weapon or item is in. This is useful because it allows you to make your favorite, or most frequently used, weapons more easily accessible.

At any time, your soldier's backpack can hold six items (including the pickaxe). That leaves five slots in which you can carry different types of guns, alternative weapons (such as Remote Explosives or Grenades), and/or powerup loot items (such as Med Kits, Chug Jugs, Shield Potions, Bandages, or Slurp Juice).

Another thing you can do from the Backpack Inventory screen is drop a weapon, loot item, or resources. Do this to free up an inventory slot in your backpack, or to share with your partner. If you drop something and your partner does not pick it up, and an enemy stumbles upon what you left behind, he or she could grab it. Select the weapon, ammo type, loot item, or resource you want to drop, and then press the Drop button. Here, one soldier is sharing a submachine gun with his partner.

If you're holding a quantity of a specific type of ammo, loot item, or resource, when you choose to drop it, this pop-up window appears. It allows you to choose how much of what you have on hand you want to share (drop). Here, the soldier had 79 wood in total, and chose to share 39 of that resource with their Duos partner.

What your soldier is currently carrying is normally shown on the right side of the screen. The location where this information is displayed will vary based on which gaming system you're using. You can always view this information. Switching to the Backpack Inventory is not always feasible, especially during an intense firefight, because you're prevented from seeing and controlling your soldier.

Whether you're playing Solo, Duos, Squads, or another *Fortnite: Battle Royale* game play mode, anytime you're visiting the island, your personal arsenal can include many different types of weapons, ranging from pistols and shotguns, to automatic weapons, rifles, and rocket launchers. In addition to these weapons, a vast and ever-changing collection of loot items is available to you.

Finding weapons and loot items and then building your arsenal is just one part of the overall challenge. You'll also need to choose the perfect weapon to use, based on the situation you're currently facing, and then ensure you have ample ammunition for that weapon. There are several different types of ammunition to collect. Remember, without ammunition, a weapon is useless. When you run out of ammo, a message that states "Not Enough Ammo" and/or "Out of Ammo!" appears on the screen, and your soldier will shake his or her head when you try to shoot.

What You Should Know About Weapons

The weapon categories firearms and explosives typically fall into include: Rifles, Grenade Launchers, Grenades, Miniguns, Pistols, Rocket Launchers, Shotguns, SMGs (Submachine Guns), and Sniper Rifles. Other types of weapons are always being introduced into the game.

Many *Fortnite: Battle Royale* gamers agree that the most useful weapon to master is any type of shotgun. There are several types of shotguns to be found within the game. They can be used in close-range or mid-range combat situations, or even at a distance. (From a distance, they're harder to aim accurately than a rifle with a scope, for example.) When using a shotgun, always try for a headshot to inflict the most damage. Each category of weapon can be used for a different purpose.

Three Tips to Improve Your Shooting Accuracy

Regardless of which weapon you're using, your aim improves when you crouch down and press the Aim button for the weapon you're using. When you press the Aim button before the trigger button, you'll zoom in a bit on your opponent, and you'll have more precise control over the positioning of the weapon's targeting crosshairs.

While it's often necessary to be running or jumping at the same time you're firing a weapon, your accuracy improves when you're standing still.

You almost always have an advantage when you're higher up than your opponent and shooting in a downward direction.

A rifle with a scope (or a thermal scope) will come in handy anytime during a match for spying on your enemies from a distance. However, conserve your ammo for this weapon until the End Game. Early on in a match, use this weapon as a fancy set of binoculars. When viewing a target through a scope, you can really zoom in from a distance.

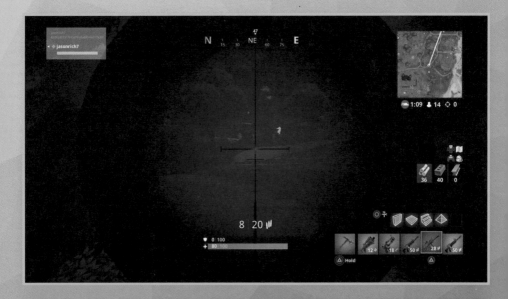

A thermal scope allows you to see through walls and spot hiding ene-mies. The yellow figure near the center of the crosshairs is an enemy soldier who is running in the distance. Using a scoped rifle allows you to shoot at your targets from a distance with extreme accuracy. One drawback to this weapon is that the time gap in between shots is long. The rifle also typically holds just a few shells (bullets) at a time before it needs to be reloaded.

Understand How Weapons Are Rated and Categorized

While every weapon has the ability to cause damage and potentially defeat your adversaries, each is rated based on several criteria, includ-ing its rarity. Weapons are color-coded with a hue around them to showcase their rarity. Remember, each type of weapon will require practice as you learn to accurately aim and use it.

Weapons with a **gray** hue are "Common."

Weapons with a **green** hue are "Uncommon."

Weapons with a **blue** hue are "Rare."

Weapons with a **purple** hue are "Epic."

"Legendary" weapons (with an **orange** hue) are hard to find, extra powerful, and very rare. If you're able to obtain one, grab it!

It is possible to collect several of the same weapon, but each could have a different rarity. So, if you collect two of the same weapon type, and one is rare, but the second is legendary, definitely keep the legendary weapon and trade the other for something else when you find a replacement.

If you're really interested in how a weapon is rated, evaluate its DPR (Damage Per Second) rating, overall Damage Rating, Fire Rate, MAG (Magazine) Capacity, and Reload Time. This is information that Epic Games tweaks often. Select a weapon when viewing your Backpack Inventory screen to see details about it.

There are plenty of websites, including: IGN.com (www.ign.com/wikis/fortnite/Weapons), Gameskinny.com (www.gameskinny.com/9mt22/complete-fortnite-battle-royale-weapons-stats-list), and RankedBoost.com (https://rankedboost.com/fortnite/best-weapons-tier-list), that provide the current stats for each weapon offered in *Fortnite: Battle Royale*, based on the latest tweaks made to the game. Just make sure when you look at this information online, it refers to the most recently released version of *Fortnite: Battle Royale*.

Choose Your Arsenal Wisely

Based on where you are, what challenges you're currently encountering, and what you anticipate your needs will be, stock your backpack with the weapons and tools you believe you'll need. Don't forget, you also need to stockpile appropriate weapons, ammo, loot items, and resources prior to the End Game.

The various types of ammunition you've collected, how much of each ammo type you have on hand, and which weapons each ammo type can be used with, is also displayed on the Backpack Inventory screen. While viewing this screen, select a specific ammunition type to learn more about it. Here you can see that Light Bullets has been selected from the Backpack Inventory screen and that this soldier has 126 of these low-caliber bullets on hand.

Some weapons, like pistols, are ideal for close-range firefights. Other weapons (like shotguns) are better suited for mid-range combat. Rifles with a scope and projectile explosive weapons (like Rocket Launchers) are ideal for destroying structures and/or enemies from a distance. It's important to find and carry an assortment of weapons, so you're able to deal with any fighting situation you encounter.

How and Where to Collect Ammo

The different types of ammunition include:

- **Heavy Bullets**—Used in sniper rifles and other high-caliber weapons that are designed for long-range shooting.
- **Light Bullets**—Used in pistols, SMGs, and most handheld guns. This type of ammo causes more damage when used at close-range. To inflict the most damage, aim for a headshot or hit your target multiple times.
- **Medium Bullets**—Used in assault rifles and similar weapons. This type of ammo is ideal for mid-range shooting, although the closer you are, the more damage each bullet will inflict.
- **Rockets**—Used with Rocket Launchers and Grenade Launchers. Even if you don't yet have one of these weapons in your personal arsenal, collect this ammo whenever you can and stockpile it. You can always share it with your partner. Having a Rocket Launcher or Grenade Launcher will be extremely useful during the End Game.
- **Shells**—Used in shotguns. This ammo will inflict the most damage at close range, but shotguns can be used when you're at any distance from your target. The farther you are away, the less damage each direct hit will inflict.

Without having the appropriate ammunition on hand, whatever weapons you're carrying will be useless. Throughout each match, there are several ways to find and collect ammo.

Ammunition can be collected from Ammo Boxes. These are scattered throughout the island, and are often found within structures on shelves or hidden behind objects. Unlike chests, they do not glow or make a sound.

Random types of ammunition can sometimes be found out in the open, lying on the ground. Sometimes the ammo is alone, but often, it's found in conjunction with a compatible weapon.

You can often grab a nice assortment of ammunition that a soldier drops, immediately after they've been defeated and eliminated from a match.

Chests, Supply Drops, and Loot Llamas often contain random collections of ammunition.

Finding, Collecting, and Using Loot Items

There are many types of loot items available to you during a match. Some are very rare, while others you'll be able to collect often. Each type of loot item serves one of four purposes.

- **Weapons**—Traps, Grenades, Stink Bombs, Impulse Grenades, and Remote Explosives are collected and then used against enemies when needed. Some of these items require an inventory slot within your backpack. Others, like Traps, get stored along with your resources. In most cases, you can carry multiples of the same item, such as three or six Grenades, within the same backpack inventory slot.
- **Tools**—Items like a Port-A-Fort or Bush can be useful to aid in your survival.
- **Health and/or Shield Powerups**—Med Kits, Chug Jugs, Bandages, Shield Potions, and Slurp Juice can be used to replenish your Health meter and/or activate and then replenish your Shield meter. Each of these items takes time to consume or use, during which time your soldier will be vulnerable to attack.
- **Transportation**—Shopping Carts, Bouncers, Launch Pads, Chillers, Rifts, and All Terrain Karts are examples of items and in-game phenomenon that can randomly be found throughout the island and that will help you travel around.

Slurp Juice is a powerup loot item you can grab and carry in your sol-dier's backpack. When it's consumed it'll replenish your soldier's Health *and* Shield meters by 25 points (up to 100 maximum), but it takes a full 25 seconds to drink it, during which time your soldier will be vulnerable to attack. Only use this item when you're somewhere safe.

A Trap is a type of weapon that you can set on almost any surface. There are several types of Traps that can be found and used on the island. When an enemy activates it, they'll receive damage and most often be defeated. Place a Trap where an enemy will stumble upon it by accident, and where it can't easily be spotted. Traps gets stored in your backpack with your resources. To set a Trap, you need to go into Building mode. Thus, Traps do not take up a slot within your backpack. You can carry multiple Traps at the same time and set them when you deem it's necessary.

Most loot items can be found within chests, Supply Drops, and Loot Llamas, as well as lying out in the open (often on the ground). Many of these items can also be acquired after you defeat an enemy—when he or she drops everything they were carrying after being eliminated from the match. Some items can also be obtained from Vending Machines (by exchanging resources you've collected within the game).

Be on the Constant Lookout for Chests, Supply Drops, and Loot Llamas

One of your first priorities once you (and your partner) land on the island is to find weapons.

Some weapons and ammo can be found lying out in the open (on the ground).

Throughout the island—mainly within buildings, homes, and other structures, as well as inside of trucks, but sometimes out in the open— you'll discover chests.

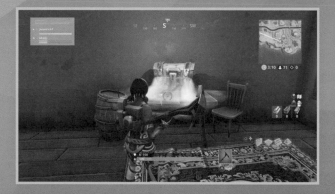

Chests have a golden glow and make a sound when you get close to them. Open chests to collect a random selection of weapons, ammo, loot items, and resources. To collect a chest's contents, you must be the first soldier to open it during a match.

Some chests are usually found at the same spot on the map match after match, although this is changing as Epic Games releases new game updates. Sometimes, chests randomly appear during each match, so always be on the lookout for them (and listen carefully for the sound they make).

As you're exploring various areas, listen closely for the unique sound chests emit. You'll often hear this sound before a chest comes into view. Assuming it's safe, approach the chest and open it. Then be ready to grab the items you want or need. Anytime you're searching a home, you'll often find one or more chests in an attic, basement, or garage. Sometimes, they're just sitting out in the open.

At random times during a match, you may be lucky enough to spot a Supply Drop. This is a floating balloon with a wooden crate attached. They're somewhat rare. If you spot one, approach with caution, and open the crate. Inside you'll discover a random selection of weapons, loot items, ammo, and resource icons.

An even rarer object to come across on the island is a Loot Llama. This colorful item looks like a piñata. Open it and you'll discover a collection of random weapons, ammo, loot items, and resource icons. Typically, the weapons found within Loot Llamas are rare and often "legendary." There are only three Loot Llamas randomly placed on the island per match.

Instead of opening a Loot Llama, an alternate strategy is to place Remote Explosives on it and then hide. As soon as an enemy soldier approaches, manually detonate the explosives to defeat the enemy. As you approach a Supply Drop or Loot Llama, consider quickly building walls around yourself and the object, so you're protected before opening the crate or smashing the Loot Llama.

Scattered randomly throughout the island are Vending Machines. Exchange resources you've collected to acquire any of the weapons or loot items being offered. Each Vending Machine offers a different selection of items that can be purchased using wood, stone, or metal. Here, Grenades are being offered in exchange for 100 wood. Like chests, Vending Machines make a unique sound when you're close to them.

GATHERING THE RESOURCES YOU'LL NEED AND BUILDING TECHNIQUES

Becoming an expert builder, especially in the heat of battle, requires practice, as well as some creativity when it comes to designing structures. Either by watching live streams of expert players on YouTube or Twitch.tv, or by staying in Spectator mode once you're eliminated from a match, watch the final stages of matches carefully to learn the best techniques for building fortresses.

To practice your building technique, travel to an unpopular and unpopulated area of the island, focus on collecting resources, and then fine tune your building skills. Experiment with different structure designs, and develop the skillset needed to be able to build very quickly, without having to think too much about it. If the Playground game play mode is currently offered (it's added and removed from the game periodically), this is the perfect place to practice building.

Each Building Tile Has Its Own Strength

There are four shapes of building tiles—vertical wall tiles, horizontal floor/ceiling tiles, ramp/stair tiles, and pyramid-shaped tiles. Once you enter into Building mode, first choose your building material. Next, choose where you want to build. Finally, one at a time, select which building tile you want to use.

Each tile has an HP level, which determines how much damage it can withstand before collapsing or being destroyed. During the building process, a tile's HP increases gradually. Wood is the fastest to build with, while working with stone is slightly slower. Metal takes the longest to build with but offers the most protection.

Each tile costs 10 of the selected resource to build. Remember, when you're in Building mode, you can't use a weapon. You'll definitely need to practice quickly switching between Combat mode and Building mode.

Here's a list of the HP strength offered by each tile type once its fully built. Keep in mind, this information could change slightly if Epic Games tweaks this aspect of the game.

TILE SHAPE	WOOD	STONE	METAL
Horizontal Floor/Ceiling Tile	140 HP	280 HP	460 HP
Vertical Wall Tile	150 HP	300 HP	500 HP
Ramp/Stairs Tile	140 HP	280 HP	460 HP
Pyramid-Shaped Tile	140 HP	280 HP	460 HP

When you go into Edit mode to alter a tile—to add a door or window, for example—the defensive strength of that tile changes. Each tile has its own HP meter which is displayed when you face the tile.

How to Become a Better Builder

The trick to becoming a highly skilled builder is speed. Achieving speed takes practice! Here are some additional strategies to help you become an expert builder.

When building a fortress, cover all sides. Don't forget to build a roof to protect yourself from assaults from above. Wood was used here.

Aside from using a Rocket Launcher from a distance to destroy part of or an entire enemy fortress, most types of mid-to-long-range shotguns and rifles will work. However, if you can sneak up on the enemy from the ground, you can attach Remote Explosives to the base of their fort or toss a few Grenades into it. This is typically quicker than continuously shooting at a fortress wall to weaken or destroy it. On the left is a basic stone fortress. The soldier tossed three Grenades through the door.

As you can see on the right, the fortress was quickly destroyed. If an enemy had been hiding out in this structure, he would have been toast.

Building an over-under ramp uses twice the resources but allows you to travel up higher (or go down from someplace high up), while protecting yourself from attacks originating from above you. As you're building a ramp, position the building cursor in the middle of the upper and lower tiles to build both at the same time.

When you need quick protection, build a vertical wall with the strongest material you have available, and then quickly build a ramp (or stairs) directly behind it. Crouch down behind this structure for protection. Doing this provides a double layer of shielding that an enemy will have to shoot through or destroy in order to reach you. Plus, by crouching down, you become a smaller target.

This is the same structure (one vertical wall with a ramp behind it), but with vertical walls built on both sides to provide extra protection from flank attacks (from the sides).

In some cases, building two ramps side-by-side gives you an advantage. An opponent who's below you can't see your exact location when you move back and forth between ramps. Also, if one ramp is about to get destroyed, quickly leap to the other to survive the attack. Yes, this requires more resources, but it's often worth it.

A "ramp rush" is a strategy that involves building a tall ramp quickly, so you're able to move directly toward and over an enemy (or their base) to initiate an attack. This strategy is commonly used during an End Game when attacking an enemy within their own fortress.

Smashing wooden pallets often generates more wood than smashing trees. However, trees provide more wood that smashing the walls, floors, and ceilings of houses or buildings. Giant trees, like those found in Wailing Woods, tend to generate the most wood. During normal combat, wood is typically the best resource to use. Save your stone and metal for fort building during the End Game.

If you see a weakness in a tall structure, and you know an enemy is at or near the top of it, shoot at that weak point. Making the structure collapse will cause your enemy to fall. A short fall will have little impact, but a fall from four (or more) levels up could be devastating.

Learn to Quickly Build "1x1" Fortresses

A 1x1 fortress is simply four walls around you, with a ramp in the center. It goes up multiple levels. Using wood allows you to build with the greatest speed, but using metal offers the greatest protection. Keep practicing until you're able to build this type of fortress very quickly.

Here's how to build a 1x1 fortress:

First build one floor tile if the ground is uneven.

Next, build four vertical walls so they surround you.

In the center of the structure, build a ramp. As the ramp is being constructed, jump on it. You've now built one level of a 1x1 fortress. Repeat these steps until the fortress has reached the desired height.

At the top, consider adding pyramid-shaped roof pieces around the top for added protection when you peek out. However, if you need protection from above as well, add a flat roof and then a pyramid-shaped roof piece directly over your head. Stone, instead of wood, was used here.

This 1x1 fortress is made of stone and is three levels tall.

Learning to edit quickly, to add windows, doors, and other customizations to a structure you've built, is an important skill to master. It takes practice to be able to edit structures at lightning-fast speed. When you're editing a wall tile, choose which of the nine squares you want to remove.

Selecting and then removing one square creates a window.

Selecting two squares (one on top of the other) creates a door. Removing two squares next to each other creates an extra wide window.

Any soldier can open and close a door that's been added to a structure. To keep enemies from following you inside your fort, consider adding a Trap inside the fortress on the bottom floor (inside the door).

Edit a floor or ceiling tile to create a hole which you can easily travel through to climb up or down a level within the structure you're building. Start by entering into Edit mode while facing a ground or ceiling tile.

Select one of the squares to remove.

Press the Confirm button to create the hole (in this case, on the floor tile).

SECTION 6

STRATEGIES THAT'LL HELP YOU AND YOUR PARTNER SURVIVE

Communication is the key to working well with your partner during a Duos match. If one player is using a gaming headset but the other is not, the person with the headset can ask the other player questions that have a "yes" or "no" answer.

The player without a headset can then respond by waving their weapon up and down for "yes," or back and forth for "no." Using the Quick Chat menu is also an option for communicating without speaking. The best situation is when you and your partner are both using gaming headsets (with a built-in microphone), so you can talk freely throughout the match.

EARLY ACCESS

LOADING..

Only YOU can prevent V-Buck Scams
Do not share your password with anyone.

You typically can't determine someone's real name, where they live, or anything about them from their username (except for how good of a gamer they are if you check their stats). However, when you're playing

Fortnite: Battle Royale with strangers (or online friends who you've never met in person), and you're both using gaming headsets with a built-in microphone so you can chat, *never* give out too much information about yourself during conversations.

Information you should not give out includes: your last name, where you're from, what school you go to, your account password, or anything else that is personal. Also, watch your language and be polite. If you bully someone online while playing *Fortnite: Battle Royale*, you'll likely be reported.

When you're unable to speak to your partner during a match, one gamer can simply follow the other and provide support as much as possible. Let the person designated as the leader decide where to go during a match, for example. While you want to stay close to your partner, don't stay too close or an enemy could take you both out at once with one explosive attack.

During this End Game, both gamers allowed their soldiers to stay very close together within their forts. Unless you're reviving your partner, it's never a good idea to stay this close and be standing still. If you do, you become an easier target for your enemies.

If you and your partner decide to launch an attack from your own fortress, an excellent strategy is for one soldier to use a Rocket Launcher or Grenade Launcher to wreak havoc on the enemy's fort. As the enemy fort begins to crumble, the other soldier can use a rifle with a scope to snipe at the enemy soldiers as they run from their fort. This strategy also works if as the enemy fort is falling apart, one or both of the enemy soldiers decide to rush your fort to launch their own attack. Using the sniper rifle, stop them in their tracks before they get too close.

Anytime you and your partner are traveling together, don't say, "There's a shooter in front of me!" Unless your partner is standing next to you and facing the same direction, this won't make any sense to him. Instead, look at the top-center of the screen and call out a compass direction instead. Say something like, "There's a shooter hiding on the bridge in the Northwest."

Whenever you're separated from your partner during a match, periodically tell them what new weapons, ammo, and loot items you've collected, and determine if your partner would benefit from items you've found but don't need. Remember, whatever you find and leave behind could be grabbed by your enemies and used against you.

If you or your partner decide to walk through a Rift, it's important to do this at the same time, or immediately one after the other. After one use, Rifts sometimes close and disappear. When this happens, one soldier will be transported a good distance away, while the other remains at their current position. As soon as you both exit the Rift and are using your glider to descend back to land, check the Location Map or the island map to determine your partner's location and travel path, so you wind up at the same place.

Anytime you and your partner are together, and you come across a chest, Supply Drop, or Loot Llama, or you're collecting what a defeated enemy has left behind, be considerate and share whatever weapons, ammo, loot items, and resources you discover. Figure out what you each need to build up and enhance your arsenals and divide up the items accordingly. As one person gathers and organizes what they're grabbing, their partner should stand guard and watch out for incoming attacks or nearby enemy movement.

As you and your partner are traveling along, if one of you spots potential danger ahead, quickly draw your weapon and hide behind something and crouch down or build up defensive walls. Pay attention to what your partner is doing and react accordingly.

There will be times when you or your partner get injured in a fire-fight, for example, and one of you needs to be revived. If you're the one who's hurt, crawl to a safe place and be sure to alert your partner if you know an enemy is close by and from which direction you were attacked. Here, the two soldiers found a stone cliff to hide behind as one partner revived the other.

If you're the one healing (reviving) your partner, approach them with caution. It's very common for an enemy to leave the soldier they've shot in a helpless position and wait for their partner to arrive before finishing off both soldiers with a surprise attack.

Make sure you and your partner are in a secure area. During the heal-ing process, you and your partner can't move around or use weapons, so you're both vulnerable to attack. As soon as the injured soldier is revived, share a Med Kit, Bandages, or another health powerup, so the soldier who was injured can regain their full health before fully entering back into a firefight.

During your island exploration, if you come across multiple powerup loot items, like Shield Potions, Med Kits, or Bandages, collect them all. Even if you don't need them, you can share them with your partner.

To share any item you're carrying—a weapon, loot item, ammunition, or resources—while you're standing close to your partner, access your soldier's Backpack Inventory screen and then highlight and select what you want to share. Press the Drop button related to the selected item. When the item drops to the ground, your partner can pick it up and add it to their own arsenal.

When traveling around the island in an ATK, decide who will drive and who will be the passenger. The passenger needs to keep their weapon handy and be ready to shoot at enemies as you approach them. It's the driver's job to use evasive driving maneuvers when incoming projectile weapons are spotted (such as missiles from a Grenade Launcher), and to choose the best route to follow to reach the intended destination. If you both need to leave the vehicle for a firefight, park the ATK near a large and sturdy object, such as a rock formation or RV that you can safely hide behind until you have time to build a defensive structure.

After defeating an enemy, don't just run to their last location to collect everything they've left behind. Don't forget, this is a Duos match, so the fallen soldier's partner could be close by. Make sure it's safe before approaching, and be ready to engage in a firefight, if necessary. In this case, one precaution you can take before approaching is to destroy the wooden structures and nearby trees that the fallen soldier's partner could be hiding in or behind.

If you get separated from your partner and don't have gaming headsets, access the island map and set a marker for the location you want to meet up at. A colored flare will be displayed for you and your partner to see.

When you can't get the height advantage over your enemy, at least try to get high enough so you're at the same height as them and then launch your attack using the most powerful weapons at your disposal. If you're using a gun to smash through walls, this will work, but it'll use up a ton of ammo. As long as your enemy has enough resources, he can keep repairing the damaged walls or rebuilding, which will cause you to waste even more ammo. Instead, wait for your enemy to peek out of their fortress and then try to hit them with a headshot using the most precise and powerful weapon you have for long-range shots.

Another common occurrence during an End Game is that the Final Circle will force you and your enemies into the same tall structure. When the final firefight happens, it'll often be the soldier or team with the fastest reflexes, the best aim, and a height advantage that wins.

You already know that basic ramps made of wood can easily be destroyed, often causing the person on the ramp to fall and get injured or defeated. It takes more resources, but consider building a reinforced ramp like these, especially during the End Game when you need to reach high levels and your enemies are skilled and well armed.

If you need to retreat from the structure you're currently in, so you can quickly reach a distant area, consider adding a Bouncer or Launch Pad to your fortress and then going airborne. Keep in mind, while you're in mid-air and traveling with your glider, an enemy can shoot at you, although you'll be a fast-moving target.

You can also use a Launch Pad or Bouncer to get away from the approaching storm, or to escape the storm if you're caught within it.

Preparing for the End Game

Not every End Game requires a soldier to build an elaborate fortress in order to win. It's more important to go into the End Game with the best possible collection of weapons, have plenty of ammunition for those weapons, and to have an abundance of resources collected so you can build ramps, protective structures, and fortresses as they're needed, based on the challenges you encounter.

Try to go into every End Game with up to 1,000 wood, 1,000 stone, and 1,000 metal. Having plenty of wood is the most important for quickly building ramps and protective walls. Being able to build a fortress from metal ensures it'll be able to withstand more damage from attacks. A Port-A-Fort or a Port-a-Fortress can be very useful during an End Game. It offers protection yet requires no resources unless you build extensions onto it or modify it.

Along with having adequate levels of resources, make sure that within your backpack's inventory, you have the loot items and weapons you'll need to launch attacks (such as a weapon with a scope and a projectile explosive weapon). Also, make sure you have ample health and shield powerups on hand. Use them in between battles that take place during the End Game, so you go into each firefight with a fully charged Health meter and Shield meter.

About halfway through each match, start thinking about the End Game and preparing for it. By defeating enemies in the later stages of a match, you're able to grab all of the weapons, ammo, loot items, and resources that they've collected. This is a great way to build your own arsenal and ensure you go into the End Game nicely equipped with resources.

As the End Game approaches, within your backpack, you ideally want to have:

- At least one sniper rifle with a scope (or thermal scope).
- At least one projectile weapon that shoots explosives, such as a Rocket Launcher or Grenade Launcher.
- Multiple Med Kits, Chug Jugs, or Bandages, so you can replenish your health. A Cozy Campfire is useful, but only if you can spare 30 seconds for it to fully work. Go into the End Game with your Health meter and Shield meter at 100.
- One or two Shield Potions to replenish your soldier's shields after each firefight. You can use one less slot in your backpack if you carry one or more Chug Jug or Slurp Juice consumables that simultaneously replenishes your soldier's health and shields.
- At least one short-range weapon and one mid-range weapon, since you'll likely need to engage in a firefight either out in the open, within your own fortress, or when you invade an enemy's fortress.
- Make sure you have plenty of ammo on hand for each type of weapon you're bringing with you into the End Game. You can sometimes collect additional weapons and ammo from defeated enemies, but it's not always safe to do this.

Twelve Additional End-Game Strategies That'll Help You Win

Here are twelve additional End-Game strategies that'll help you win:

1. If you're going to build a mighty fortress during the End Game, choose the best location to build it. This will likely be where you'll make your final stand in battle. Keep in mind, if you're in the dead-center of the Final Circle, you will become the center of attention, which probably isn't good.

2. Make sure your fortress is tall, well-fortified, and that it offers an excellent, 360-degree view of the surrounding area from the top level.

3. If your fortress gets destroyed, be prepared to move quick, and have a backup strategy in place that will help to ensure your survival. Having the element of surprise for your attacks gives you a tactical advantage. Don't become an easy target to hit. Keep moving around your fort, or while you're out in the open!

4. During the End Game, don't engage every remaining player. Allow them to fight amongst themselves to reduce their numbers, plus reduce or even deplete their ammo and resources.

5. Only rely on a sniper rifle (or scoped rifle) to make long-range shots if you have really good aim and a clear line of sight to your enemy. Otherwise use explosive weapons that'll cause damage over a wide area. A Rocket Launcher, for example, is ideal. This type of weapon will damage or destroy an enemy fortress, plus injure or defeat an enemy soldier who is inside.

6. Always keep tabs on the location of your remaining enemies during the End Game. Don't allow them to sneak up behind you, for example. If you lose track of an enemy who you know is nearby, listen carefully for their movement.

7. Don't invest a lot of resources into a massive and highly fortified fortress until you know you're in the Final Circle during a match. Refer to the map and the displayed timer.

Otherwise, when the storm expands and moves, you could find it necessary to abandon your fort, and then need to build another one quickly, in a not-so-ideal location. Having to rebuild will use up your resources.

8. Base pushers are enemies that aren't afraid to leave their fortress and attempt to attack yours during the final minutes of a match. Be prepared to deal with their close-range threat. Thanks to tweaks made to the game, it's no longer necessary to build an elaborate fortress to win a match.

9. If two or three enemies remain, focus on one at a time. Determine who appears to be the most imminent and largest threat. Be prepared to change priorities at a moment's notice, based on the actions of your enemies.

10. Some final battles take place on ramps, not from within fortresses. In this situation, use speed and quick reflexes to get higher up than your enemy. At this point, having accurate aim with the proper weapon is the key to winning. Try to destroy the bottom of an enemy's ramp to make the whole thing come crashing down. The soldier standing on the ramp will be injured or defeated, based on how far he or she falls to the ground.

11. If you need to revive your partner during the End Game, make sure you build walls around yourself. When your enemies don't see any movement for 10 to 15 seconds, they may assume you're busy reviving your partner and move in quickly to attack while you're both vulnerable.

12. Study the live streams created by expert *Fortnite* players (on YouTube and Twitch.tv) to learn their End-Game strategies and see how they react to various challenges.

FORTNITE: BATTLE ROYALE RESOURCES

On YouTube (www.youtube.com) or Twitch.TV (www.twitch.tv/directory /game/Fortnite), in the Search field, enter the search phrase "*Fortnite: Battle Royale*" to discover many game-related channels, live streams, and pre-recorded videos that'll help you become a better player.

Also, be sure to check out these other online resources:

WEBSITE OR YOUTUBE CHANNEL NAME	DESCRIPTION	URL
Fandom's *Fortnite* Wiki	Discover the latest news and strategies related to *Fortnite: Battle Royale*.	http://fortnite.wikia.com/wiki/Fortnite_Wiki
FantasticalGamer	A popular YouTuber who publishes *Fortnite* tutorial videos.	www.youtube.com/user/FantasticalGamer
FBR Insider	The *Fortnite: Battle Royale Insider* website offers game-related news, tips, and strategy videos.	www.fortniteinsider.com
Fortnite Gamepedia Wiki	Read up-to-date descriptions of every weapon, loot item, and ammo type available within *Fortnite: Battle Royale*. This Wiki also maintains a comprehensive database of soldier outfits and related items released by Epic Games.	https://fortnite.gamepedia.com/Fortnite_Wiki
Fortnite Intel	An independent source of news related to *Fortnite: Battle Royale*.	www.fortniteintel.com

Fortnite Scout	Check your personal player stats, and analyze your performance using a bunch of colorful graphs and charts. Also check out the stats of other *Fortnite: Battle Royale* players.	www.fortnitescout.com
Fortnite Stats & Leaderboard	This is an independent website that allows you to view your own *Fortnite*-related stats or discover the stats from the best players in the world.	https://fortnitestats.com
Game Informer Magazine's *Fortnite* Coverage	Discover articles, reviews, and news about *Fortnite: Battle Royale* published by *Game Informer* magazine.	www.gameinformer.com/search/searchresults.aspx?q=Fortnite
GameSkinny Online Guides	A collection of topic-specific strategy guides related to *Fortnite*.	www.gameskinny.com/tag/fortnite-guides/
GameSpot's *Fortnite* Coverage	Check out the news, reviews, and game coverage related to *Fortnite: Battle Royale* that's been published by GameSpot.	www.gamespot.com/fortnite
IGN Entertainment's *Fortnite* Coverage	Check out all IGN's past and current coverage of *Fortnite*.	www.ign.com/wikis/fortnite
Jason R. Rich's Website and Social Media Feeds	Share your *Fortnite: Battle Royale* game play strategies with this book's author and learn about his other books.	www.JasonRich.com www.FortniteGameBooks.com Twitter: @JasonRich7 Instagram: @JasonRich7
Microsoft's Xbox One *Fortnite* Website	Learn about and acquire *Fortnite: Battle Royale* if you're an Xbox One gamer.	www.microsoft.com/en-US/store/p/Fortnite-Battle-Royalee/BT5P2X999VH2
MonsterDface YouTube and Twitch.tv Channels	Watch video tutorials and live game streams from an expert *Fortnite* player.	www.youtube.com/user/MonsterdfaceLive www.Twitch.tv/MonsterDface

(continued on next page)

Ninja	Check out the live and recorded game streams from Ninja, one of the most highly skilled *Fortnite: Battle Royale* players in the world on Twitch. tv and YouTube.	www.twitch.tv/ninja_fortnite_hyper www.youtube.com/user/NinjasHyper
Nomxs	A YouTube and Twitch.tv channel hosted by online personality Simon Britton (Nomxs). He too is one of *Fortnite*'s top-ranked players.	https://youtu.be/np-8cmsUZmc or www.twitch.tv/videos/259245155
Official Epic Games YouTube Channel for *Fortnite: Battle Royale*	The official *Fortnite: Battle Royale* YouTube channel.	www.youtube.com/user/epicfortnite
Turtle Beach Corp.	This is one of many companies that make great quality, wired or wireless (Bluetooth) gaming headsets that work with all gaming platforms.	www.turtlebeach.com

Your *Fortnite: Battle Royale* Adventure Continues . . .

Playing Duos matches is fun, and it allows you to rely on your partner to help defeat your enemies and overcome the challenges imposed by the island itself. When you have a partner, it's important to work together in order to achieve success, since all of your enemies will be partnered up as well (at least during the early stages of a match, before soldiers start getting eliminated).

Experiencing Duos matches with strangers is a great way to learn new strategies, as well as improve your fighting and building skills. However, *Fortnite: Battle Royale* offers several other game play modes that are equally fun and challenging.

To keep you on your toes, Epic Games regularly updates *Fortnite: Battle Royale* by introducing new weapons, loot items, and points of interest on the map. It also tweaks how much damage can be caused by specific weapons and certain loot items, so even if you become a pro at fighting in a certain location, or using a specific weapon to continuously win firefights, you'll likely be forced to modify your strategies as new game updates are introduced.

Whichever game play mode you choose to experience, to become a truly skilled *Fortnite: Battle Royale* player will require a lot of practice. Be patient and don't allow yourself to get frustrated if you frequently wind up being eliminated from matches and have trouble achieving #1 Victory Royale. Keep working to perfect your fighting, building, and even your ATK driving skills, as you become acquainted with each of the island's points of interest.

Always try to learn from your mistakes and learn as much as possible from the other gamers you partner up with in Duos mode, for example. In situations when you're clearly a better gamer than your partner, teach them what you know and help them out. Remember, the most important thing is to have fun!